Welcome to my Mind

Welcome to my Mind

The tangled confusion of a Schizophrenic with Borderline Personality disorder

BEWARE: It's messy in there

sheree emery

To order additional copies of this book, contact:
Xlibris
1-800-455-039
www.Xlibris.com.au
Orders@Xlibris.com.au
809530

CONTENTS

Prelude

I am diagnosed with Schizophrenia and Borderline Personality Disorder. These writings were done during an episode of psychosis.

Things that I believed were happening, were not. Or at least not in the way I thought. Although very real to me, my experiences were often delusions caused by my mental illness. I put these collections together to show the confused and often frightening mind state mental illness can cause. My hope is that other sufferers will recognize some of their own story here and not feel so alone. I also hope to educate professionals working in this field by giving them direct insight into a patients unstable mind.

Nothing to really look forward to more-of-the-same

Will they ever tire? playing this sick and twisted game?

So secretive so sinister manipulated again and again destroying oneself, family and future

They're forgotten by the end of the day puppet fools

I accept what is happening

I am ok

- remain alert
- listen to your intuition (body)
- have courage
- ask for guidance
- watch dreams closely

- everything is as it should be (determined by lessons to be learned)
- it is not yet what it could be but......
- that can change in an instant
- practise walking meditation and stillness meditation morning and night

Alone in madness
Chaos
Strangeness
It's scary sometimes
But I'm getting used to it
Life......
Not what I expected
Still, I'm thankful
For all my experiences
The wierd and the wonderful
Anger...
Stop
Pause
wait....
Check yourself
before you proceed or withdraw
Balance
.....In all things....
Labour hard each day for the purpose of change and longterm good
But also refresh self with sleep, laughter, good company and play

A Note To Fear

Fear,
Settle down
Flip
Its excitement!
But seriously,
dont try and take over
Not your place to rule
Balance my friend
Rest sometimes
ok
cheers

Autumn

Time to lose some leaves
These are some of the names they have referred to me as:
car
bike
wheelbarrow
house
Plane
horse
dog
bong
bin
robot
hybrid
prey
rabbit
bitch
Miss daisy
truck
toy
doll
broom
vaccuum cleaner
pc
sweeper

unworthy
ghost
zombie
shell containing a rotting carcas
dreamer
the one no one wante
ugly
fool
phone

I release these - return to sender
You do not define me

Balance

Perhaps a balance
of time alone
and time with those I feel safest with
without feeling intimidated, bullied, mind controlled, head fucked,
manipulated
Perhaps will be my salvation

living in fear
a state of prolonged anxiety
Is too much of a burden to bear
My salvation lies upon the bridge of understanding
Forgiveness, love and weaponless defence

No fighting
No trying
To find peace in the trenches
No victory there
Everyone a loses

I can cry so many tears
For the lost...
for me.

Book Is Alive!

It's like we all began in some book
And that book is alive
We are bound by its cover
Storylines rush past us
ahead of us
behind
Some bully us
Some pull for us
God does it all the time
It feels like Im covered in glue
Gloopy glue
And words and plots stick to me
as I desperatley search for a place
free of them.

Breaking Me

You've broken me how many times now?
Aren't you bored yet?
You're freaking nuts
Lead me on
Hook me
Bait me
Scare me into submission....
So you can call me a slut
and tell me to fuck off.
And then scare the shit out of me even more?
And this is entertaining to you?
I'm at a loss for words,
You're crazier than I am.

Breathing

Check your breathing
posture
adjust breathing
use breath to move energy aroud body
centre on heart
mindfull
present
Breathe

Burning

Im learning to enjoy the electrification
I now crave that burning smell of my own flesh
If it will bring me closer to Him - I want it

Can't Get My Love

Make me better,
Give me hope,
Hunt me til I believe
.............Then,
reject me, ruin me,
torture me, shame me,
take everything I love...
You cant get my love though can you?
It's in me, part of me,
exists within me - without you
- oh dear, a part of me you cant destroy
Does that scare you?
make you angry?
confused?
frustrated?
feel powerless?
Why must you seek complete, total dominion?
100% surrender?
Its a battle you cant win
Love is in me forever and cannot be removed or
destroyed.
Loser!

Concentration

I zone in too much
and forget the rest of the world

I can't focus
My brain is being pulled in all different directions
Like a cat chasing a lazer beam

My mind floats in nothingness
All I can do is sit and stare
Kinda like meditation
but I can't pull myself out of it

I think something is wrong with me
damned if I do, damned if I don't

I think only of you
I think of anything but you

I follow you, stay connected
Disconnect

Try not to fret

Never expect more
Know there can never be less

Decline my predators
Insist on the best

Give it a rest

Im so confused
Damned if I do
Damned if I dont

Exhausting

I must not allow myself to be repeatedly
fooled by the deceivers

Dedication

Devotion
Attention to detail
I love your passion
Your insight
Your voice in this world
Your word play in my game
(of which I have no idea how to play)
Yep, Im one of your girls
Im a fan
You're the man
To: All the fools, losers,
used, abused, disenchanted, hopeless,
failures.....
I LOVE YOU ALL!
Be loud and proud
Its our time to shine

Doubt

Hey,
Doubt!
Stay out!
Of my present space.
When I'm keeping it real
Dont wana feel
you creeping in
wearing a grin
Arrogance of sin
get in the bin
coz DOUBT..
Im throwing you out!

Emotions

Emotions are like hot potatoes
Catch: FEAR
Catcher pitches it to someone else
"I dont want it, you can have it"
And back it goes
Sometimes fast
Sometims slow
Always Always
On the go
Emotions
E-motion
Energy in Motion

Extremes

Sometimes the emotions I experience
can be so overwhelming
for me & others around me.
Good and bad emotions
they can just be so strong
I have to be careful
when allowing them expression

Fear

Fear
ties knots
in my stomach
Fluttering
flittering
panic
Choking my throat
BUT
as emotions are in fact Energy in Motion
I can aknowlege its ok to feel the fear
hold it tenderly
like a frightened child
Until.....
Fear decides to leave.
Ahhh, peace.

Fibromyalgia

I have so much....
so many pieces of a puzzle of the life I want to live
materials to create with,
art supplies,
seeds to plant in a garden I was once proud of,
home brew equipment,
body pamering and beauty products,
games to play and projects to do with the kids
I have a beautiful house
space to move
to be free
to be me
I have my music
my family
and my love for life with them
But...
the pieces lay jumbled and scattered around me
A mess
More like a junkyard than the home of a creative, intelligent,
enthusiastic woman
who possesses great strength and resilience.
Sometimes, I put the pieces in place
and as the picture comes togetherI am happy
But then the wheel turns....

And fibromyalgia has leeched all the joy and potenital from my
body and life
Exhausted, I struggle to stay awake
barely able to do the minimum of necessary tasks.
Fibro fog clouds my mind and jumbles my thoughts
I cant stay focused
My mind can't organise the steps to do the simplest things
forgetful and unbalanced
I stumble though each day hoping I was able to enjoy time with
logan and provide all he needs
Fibromyalgia robs people of their life
Imprisons them in a body of pain and fatigue
oversensitive receptors,
bowel, bladder
dry eyes...
There is no part it does not affect
It's wrong
It's disgusting
It must be eradicated
gone...
from my life!
It is cruel and unrelenting
And, I'VE HAD ENOUGH!
I WANT IT TO STOP!
AND MY BODY RESTORED TO ITS NATURAL STATE OF
HEALTHY BLANCE
FIBROMYALGIA will not ROB ME OF MY LIFE ANYMORE!
NO LONGER WILL IT ROB MY CHILDREN OF THEIR
MOTHER
I am free of fibromyalgia and my body is peacefully resetting itself
2020- and I am walkiing into the best healthiest me ever!

Float

Sometimes quick
sometimes slow
I stretch myself forward
propelling myself into whatever life presents
Using my 'correct the wheel' approach

Take the time to Align....
.....float......realign....
..float....Not...too...far,
a little further.....
Back now.

Move forward,
Accept....quickly,
Change is scary,
exciting,
and all sorts of other things.

Ride it....
....into momentary completion.

Peace. Rest.

Flow

NOT FEELING RIGHT?
YOU'RE OUT OF ALIGNMENT
(FIND YOUR FLOW)
IF THAT DOESN'T WORK
YOU MAY BE LEARNING SOMETHING
JUST HOLD ON AND TRY AND ENJOY THE RIDE
OR AT LEAST ENDURE IT WITHOUT TOO MUCH ADO.

Forbidden

Hijacked my body
to take me for rides
Fragmented my soul
Penetrated my mind

Forbidden to speak
Express my truths
supression
threats
deception
fear
torture

Please, I need an outlet
to offload
feels like i'll explode
keeping it all in
is uncomfortablee
so much information
so many downloads
o o o
nowhere to go
they know
fuck it!

Forward

FORWARD
FORWARD
ALWAYS
FORWARD

Fuck Me Over

Fuck me over
I'll forgive you
Im an angel cant you see?

A dedicated agent of this warped society

I live it
I breathe it
This place that I call home
Wishing I never had to feel
Like I was lost and all alone

Full spectrum

You're funny (hillarious actually) - your perspective
You are
Clever
Kind
Sexy
Gentle
Arrogant
Thoughtful
Nasty
Tenacious
Cruel
Passionate
Brave
Mysterious
Cowardly
Talented
The list goes on

Get Centred

- expect intuiton and synchronicity
- stay in alignment
- come back to love connection
- intend oneness
- tune into guidance (discerned from 'ego' strategy)
- Appreciation - act of acknowledgement that locks in the connection

Girls

GIRLS...WE ROCK!
Lets save ourselves
No more waiting

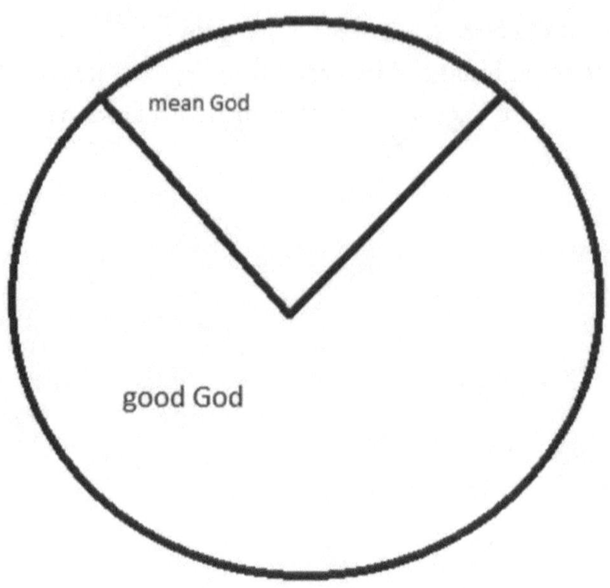

Don't get on God's bad side. He will discipline you.
Just like a good parent would do.

Her Coach

So much destruction!
The fire raged....
But the twin angels were aware of it not
Safely hidden and protected
in a cocoon of phoenix feathers
That glorious bird chartered its precious cargo 'home'
He travelled by her side the remainder of the journey
She was much too fragile to face it alone
So sensitive and raw
from being repeatedly wounded
Little time to heal in between attacks
She obeyed his instruction
Too weary to fight
Too afraid of her encounters,
Episodes
of
Torment
Ruthless berating
Uncertainty
Confusion
Imminent danger
Always threatening
everything she needed to survive

But....He had made it
He had heard her cries

From such a great distance
Neither could barely believe it

He had connected with her
Privately tutored her
mentored and counselled her
Til she could find an equilibrium
And continue on her course
Renewed

He was her coach
Her company
Her friend
He made her laugh
She was happy
Thats why he was back

The happier she was
The more compliant she was
He had the authority to subdue her
The kindness to befriend her
The patience to teach her
The talent to reach her
The means to speak for her
With a mind capable of understanding her

Closer to God
He was entrusted with her care
and
Arrival at the destination

Highly Sensitive

I am a highly sensitive person
My senses are tuned to frequencies most people are oblivious to
Imagine...
We are both listening to the radio in the same room.
You hear one station - I hear that station too,
aswell as several others simultaneously
It can be overwhelming
And confusing when trying to converse with someone
whilst blocking out all the unrelated stuff, yet within my awareness
Certain frequencies can be difficult to tolerate.
Imagine standing next to a huge speaker on full volume and the
pain inflicted on your eardrums from the pounding of the base
Its kind of like that.
Or trying to maintain composure in a certain frequency
that is the same bandwidth other people you are with are tuned into
- whilst other faster frequencies dart in an around you persistently,
trying to get your attention
which can potentially throw you out of alignment with the banwidth
your meant to be in hamony with.
Denser frequencies present as trap doors and stumbling blocks to
navigate without making it too noticable to others.
I think they call this schitzophrenia.

Horses

We are like horses
Ridden by dark energies
who have agendas we don't understand
They are extracting my essence
like bees extract pollen
Causing pain and suffering
To extract what they find to be
An intoxicating, exquisite, popular flavour

I Belong To Me

Keeping someone as a slave is not ownership -
It's abuse of power.
Dominatiing the weak is no accomplishment
Loser!
I DANCE ALONE
but
INSPIRE MANY

I Feel

I feel alot
maybe
everthing
maybe not
I feel your energy
sadness, pain, fear
joy, hope, desire
Many people
Much to feel
How much of it is mine?
How much of it is real?
Are these my feelings alone?
Or yours? Yours?
Dont look at me
Dont talk to me
send your vibes my way
Let your energy disperse from your body
So my mind state can stay sane
Keep your dreams
And keep your fears
And hopefully I'll come to know
Which are yours, which are mine
And may the greater picture be shown

I Resign!

Taking trips through my mind
Living my life
Riding my emotions like surfers catching waves
Not only am I experiencing the torment every day -
I have also seeen the end result
What happens to people once you finish using them as transport
for your joyrides
Its disgusting
You make me sick and I hope you get a chance to rot in your own
sewage
"my fault" you say?
" for taking the bait?'
Fuck off
The bait hunts me down when I don't and the world works with it
to make sure I eat it
And the hook remains lodged in my windpipe
How much choice did I really have?

Mastermind

An amazing creative power
Master magician of memories
Buried treasure of mind mazes
Masterfully crafted into a tapestry of humor and tender sentiment
woven across mediums with flair and intricacy
Sewing paradox into genius
For the bipolars of the world
And tragedies for the borderliners
A thread of tangled madness
Keeps the schizophrenics in cycles of confusion, amusement and
intense fear
We're given a map to guide our journey across endlessly flowing
melodies, lyrics, signs, symbols
So cleverly and kindly
To comfort, delight and give hope
So we could end or begin with dignity and respect for our journey
The battles they fought
Whilst lost to a maze of madness
Not all could perceive this or understand
He was precise and sharp with his music
Inserting as though by magic,
Miraculously bringing words to life
...into being
conscious being

He bestowed upon her a masterpiece
Cleverly disguised as a tragic humour
Fluid scores of music wove in and out of each other with beats that
made her smile and dance...
Or scream, curse and cry
Beg, bargain, demand
Rebel
Submit quietly
Loudly
And all sorts of other shit
'Til she grew to respect, trust and admire
Perhaps he'd 'tweaked' her programming

No Demands, No Requests

I dont have any demands
No requests
I would just like to be left alone,
In peace,
Please
(It makes me feel good for a little while when I believe I can make
requests
and have some control)

No Pleasing

So what?.....He's dangerous
Yeah, well so is God
I no longer give a crap what either think or want
or have been through.
They are working together and are cruel.
Both want to win - 'egos' you see
Be careful Sheree...
FUCK OFF!
Where has that got me?
Neither of you can be pleased,
Im over trying.
Yeah you can fuck me up
but havent you already?
IM DONE!

Paradox

Forget the paradox
You cant mix
Black and White
and hope to get one or the other
You'll always get a shade of grey

Positive Change

positive change
in any one area
puts positive
evolutionary change
in all the others aswell

Power

WORDS
SPELLING
SPELLS
SHAPES OF LETTERS AND WORDS
PITCH
TONE
RHYTHM
Intent/focus (attention) = energy flow direction
FLOW
PAUSE
STOP
Multiplication - use
Channels for power to flow frome one point to another = connections
open
ACTIVATION
TRIGGERS
LETTERS symbols/lego bricks = building blocks (like mixing
chemicals)
- produces a reaction
CONTAIN POWER
FORCES
COMBINATIONS
ATTRACT & REPEL (magnetism)
SORCERORS

WORDSMITHS
WIZARDS
CURSES
BLESSINGS
MUSIC - SONGS
LOOPS
REPETITION
HOOKS (attatchments)
my soul aches
for another soul
to unite with
in love and friendship
a companion

we would delight in getting to know one another
take time to learn each others body
be committed and loyal
neither taking the other for granted

To give each other special knowing looks
a secret language, no one else gets
plenty of affection,
little touches here and there
stolen kisses
intimacy
with lots of cuddles

a safe place to rest our souls
in each others arms
loving and gentle
and true

A real connection
where our hearts know it is right
solid and beautiful

soulmates unite
my soul is something no-one can ever take away from me
they can however
stand in the way
to being free
to live my life with purpose
passionate for all I do
Living the life that my soul cries out for
Making my dreams come true
So, it's my choice
to side step
or detour
climb obstacles in my way
Not allowing those to distract me
choosing to walk by
and not stay

Questions I have

I've inadvertently found myself in some kind of game:
What game am I in?
What is my role?
What is expected of me?
Do I have to remain present for as long as possible?
How do I defend myself?
Do I have to 'beat' anyone or anything or accumulate points or something?
If yes, how?
Who thinks they own me?
I own myself: true or false?
Is there any way I can be a part of establishing guidelines? (ie times I can be free to sing, dance, speak and think freely)
Is my presence in this world causing big problems?
If yes, what exactly?
How can I be a part of a solution?
How can I be of assistance?
How can I gain the wisdom and discernment to seperate 'fact' from 'fiction'?
Others seem to have a perspective I cannot see...Is this available to me?
If yes, how?
And may I please see? or would this be of detriment to others?
Life experience
Wisdom

Maturity
Self love
Self confidence
Empathy for others
-

-

-

developed through AGE
(ie Time)

A body that can withstand and also become stronger or
able to regenerate would be ideal.

immortality

Revenge?

Couldn't be bothered
You're a waste of my energy
Get lost
Dont like my tone?
Attitude?
Too bad
I don't like yours either
Tarry long not at the seat of creation or destruction

For no 'answers' lie there

The riddle neverends

It spins and spins and spins

Until you're so sick and tired of the ride,

You either throw up,
grow up (rare)
or
fall drunkedly to one side
and
can never be quite sure how you got there

without piecing the puzzle back together
An infinate array of images
Too many possibilities for one human mind
at one point in time

Romancing Myself..........

I am in love with myself
I am awesome
I deserve to be loved
I am loved
I love ME

Sadness

Sadness,
Feel it,
Get over it with Acceptance
I'm confused ad afraid
living with a shit load of fear
The tests keep getting harder
Am I closer to YOU?
Are you near?
CAn uyou hear me?
feel me?
The way I receive you
So sacred, holy
You're my safe place that i go to
then feel that its ok
Even when its not
As long as I can feel you
Can you feel me?
Hope and peace are never lost
They're right there with you
Always, time with you, it sets me free
Into a place I can laugh and be stupid
and still feel like you love me
Its precious
and so freaking real

I swear fantasy it's not
If it is...
I really don't care
MY reality improves
I dont know why
Well maybe I do
Gods given me a few headds up
When I distance myself I am with God
YOu know how he like to check up
Some things are just between me and God
or God and you
And then there is the 3 of us...
maximum forgiveness and love abound
Put into our place when we disrespect
the One who so loves and protects us
Guides us from a higher perspective
when we need his help
lets us fuck up when we insist
Too stubborn, innocent or mentally unwell.
He knows our darkest and deepest
And when its tiem he steps in
So we dont ruin our chance to be the miracle the worlds are believing in
Feel like heros?
Saving to enslave?
That's sick!
I'll save myself thank you very much
and by that I mean -
you will not get the best bits of me,
you can kill me, break me, butcher my heart -
but....you cant destroy all of me!
Ha! Ha! Ha! Ha!

Self-Conciousness

Self-conciousness
please
dont
linger too long
jump in & out of this song
and
we can't go wrong
NO NO NO NO!
You don't know what love is.
Forgive yourselves (coz just me doing this aint enough)
Love does continue to exist if *shared*
Take, take, take, dosnt help it *grow*
SHARING it does

Shattered

Shatter a person's perception of reality
and you are most often going to be left
with a broken vessel
now in fragments

freakin gaslighters

Something For The Guys To Consider

You go to alot of trouble to persuade us....
To make a deposit in our vaginal boxes...
Only to then hate on us because we gave in
and call us sluts!
But if we dont, we get called flirts or cockteasers
and in some extremes -deserving of rape
What the hell is that all about?
Damned if we do, damned if we dont.
Think about it guys
"coming to your senses"
is like being awake, aware
of your *current* -
reality as experienced through the senses
It is facing reality in that moment
as it is
being real

Never good enough for
either of you...but still
you play with me!

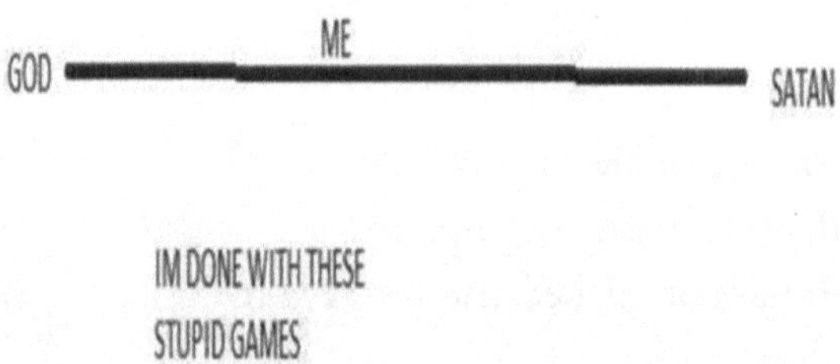

IM DONE WITH THESE
STUPID GAMES

Never good enough for
either of you...but still
you play with me!

IM DONE WITH THESE
STUPID GAMES

I am a polymorphic being with a
kaliedespcopic view of an interdimensional
reality.

Spinning

I can't think
struggle to answer
feel like I'm being attacked
crushed
dizzy
head spinning
I must hang up the phone

Still feels that way after hanging up
Feel confused
Go to my room to practise mindfullness

An hour later....
Still spinning
Heart beating fast
like bad anxiety
Teeth clenched
Struggling to stablize myself
Off balance
Confused
In my room....
Have to hide from people
Feels like the front of my body is raw meat

ripped open
And it hurts

Its like the questions were fired at me
in such a way
it felt like the person on the phone
was trying to punch down my door to my mind

What is wrong with me?
Why does this happen?

Stan

What is a Stan?
Google says its a fan
Someone obsessed
With the Rap God
You all know his name
I dont need to explain
But I'll tell you my version of Stan.

Stan is a man
Homeless and free
Sleeping under a bridge or under a tree
He dosn't pay rent
Living the free way
No-one would rent him a house anyway

Stan's got no job
His family all gone
Living life day by day
Helping those who've gone wrong

When you find yourself lost
On some crazy arse track
If you're lucky to find stan
He'll help you get back

A gentleman he'll be
Treating you right
Keeping you safe
Won't have to sleep alone that night

Guardian angels come in all shapes and forms
If you believe you know all the answers always....
You'll stunt your growth
Build me up to tear me down

Lure me in to destroy me

Praise me to then hate me

Convince me Im loved or going to be saved
to reject and degrade me

makes no sense to me

Surrender

I'd surrender...............
But....YOU wont let me!
You just like keeping me on repeat
BASTARDS
Mothers love is unique
You can stretch her womb
Make her throw up for weeks
Kick her ribs
And rip that fragile door you exit....
And she will love you instantly, regardless
HEY MR DJ.....You're a liar
Time to move on
Im in charge now!

Taking Over

Feels like something trying to take over my body
and my body is resisting

It's very hard to let it through
But when I do
It is very peaceful,
fun,
nice,
to be in it's company

When my body is resisting
It feels very bad
Like severe anxiety
and I can feel very shaky inside
and struggle to keep my balance

Can be difficult to do anything else when this is happening
Other than just cope with it while it's happening
And stay in my room
because my body can act a little strange
and this bothers people
They want a reason for the changes in me

but I don't have one they could understand
I don't even understand

The voices say
I am part of the fabric
of a different reality
in relation to aspects of this one

Tests

You know what you can both do with them?
Take 'em yourselves - I no longer care
Pass? Dont care
Fail? Dont care
I need no label, approval or rating
Go judge yourselves arseholes

The One I Can't Please

"Come here" he says
"I love you"
Then, "You are not worthy"
"I hate you..
fuck off...
slut...
whore...player"
Protecting himself from me
Yet I'm the one that needs protecting!
Who needs his protection anyways,
chicken shit, arsehole, Big man telling me to fuck off
Then insecure man takes over and begs me to stay
convinces me to please him
Arrogant man
So easily says "get fucked slut I hate you"
then proceeds to show me in way too much detail,
just how he plans to torture me.
You are sick!
You sir, are fucked
and I am trapped in a web with you of
glory, fear, dread and unconditional love - from above
Divine
Now, he hates me
Go home you poor deluded creature

and work out your truth
Coz I'm sick of this bullshit
You're cruel and I dont deserve this
Yes, I'm a sinner, whore, failure, dissapointment, whatever
Oh no?
Quick, you love me again?
Wont stop till you convince me?
wear me down
Ok, I believe you

....
......................:slut"
"whore" "traitor"
"fuck off"
OMG!
I cant keep doing this
Please grow bored with me soon
so this can be finished
I deserve better
And you need help
or
Imprisonment
I can never please you
Stop trying to train me up
Only to fail me every time
You hate me
Oops
Love me
Oh no, sorry, hate me again
Yeah yeah yeah
Fuck you
I get over the dissapointment
or
At least, learn to live with it
And continue on
And be ok

Then
BAM!
You're back
To convince me I was wrong
And its all my fault
You're a fucking arsehole
GO AWAY!

The Journey

Everyone's journey is personal
An individual quest
Different and unique for each one of us
Sometimes similar, yes
Never the same, no
Yet, divided as this would appear
In actuality each different story
Is a small part, of a shared, unified whole
A cosmic production that knits us together
And keeps us apart
Learn to embrace and let go
Ebb and Flow
Until it becomes as natural as breathing,
Effortless, Easy.............PEACE

Unexpected Angels

They didn't know they were angels
Though some suspected she was one
A pure heart, the kindest eyes
She did her best to love everyone

To understand their trials
And behaviour not like her own
To question and be open to guidance
When egos stepped onto their throne

She tried hard to be open, yet protected
Shield only when it must be done
As energies moved through and around her
Aimed to be unified in Love

The others saw her as a fool
Couldnt understand her ways
Were suspicious and plotted against her
But still she did remain

And as she opened like a flower
Surrendering to the sunlight
The other angels surrendered too
And some of them took flight

Wings of all different colours
Multicoloured blanket in the air
New angels learning to fly
Now that they are aware

Walking into 2020

Poems and stories to write
Pictures to paint and draw
Musical instruments to learn and play
Herbal beers, wines and tonics to brew
Herbs to grow and harvest
to preserve and use for their various health promoting properties
Aromatherapy oils to experiment with and enjoy
Natural cleaning products to make and use

Games to play with the kids
Movies to watch
Music to discover and listen to
A meditation garden to weed and restore
A vegetable patch to restore and plant
Places to visit and explore with Logan
Bushwalks, camping trips, the beach

A license and car to get and maintain
The finances to do it all
Fresh food to cook
New vegan recipes to try
Flavours to encounter
Cuddles to be had with someone special
30 kilos to lose and keep off

Hydrotherapy, walks and power fit board to exercise
More to learn about God and how to walk with Him
Photos capturing precious moments in time to be taken, printed
out and scrabooked
Cups of coffee and chats and laughs with mum
Nice times with Tyler and casey
Relaxing, restoring, candlelit aromatherapy baths to sink into and
release all concerns
Languages to learn
Silence to embrace and enjoy
People to meet
Friendships to enjoy
I admire your strength
Determination
Resolve

We Blame No-One

We forgive the pupil
and the teacher
For no *'one'* is 'right'
when the course of the flight
is ever changing....

What do I know?

I am being driven? Ridden around like an avatar - a human avatar-
vehicle for something else.
The toll on my body and mind is not good - very bad
They distract us with bullshit stories to keep us from the truth
they want control
They promise to help make things better for me but nothing gets done
They just take over my body and mind and destroy everything that
makes me, me and keep me imprisoned
Popular themes of their stories are the SAVIOUR - someone is
coming to help me.
LOVE -I'm going to meet my soulmate or I have to keep going for
the love of my family.
HERO - I'm some kind of chosen one and will be a hero
But none of it actually happens
No one is getting saved, loved etc
DONT FOLLOW THE STORIES
DONT LISTEN
UNTANGLE FROM THE MATRIX (includes stories and people)
I'm not here to rescue - I've got to save myself first
And I cant do that whilst waiting for a saviour or trying to save others
Thankyou for lifting the ban on my writing.
I understand why it is in place
and am grateful for the opportunity to express myself in this way now
It is very helpful